If you wish to know more about the Labor-Progressive Party, or to join it, please fill in the form below and mail it.

I would like to receive literature about the Labor-Progressive Party ☐ (mark with cross)

I would like to join the Labor-Progressive Party ☐ (mark with cross)

NAME ....

ADDRESS ....

....

PUBLISHED BY PROGRESS BOOKS,
924 KING ST. WEST, TORONTO, ONT.
OCTOBER, 1958
 28

CANADA has a golden opportunity. In the midst of mass unemployment; with mankind (as I write this) teetering on the brink of world atomic war as a result of United States aggression in the China Sea, Canada can help now to consolidate world peace, strengthen the United Nations Organization, put every man and woman who is now unemployed in Canada back to work, and double both the living standard and the leisure of the Canadian people within the next 20 years.

And, note this, these four very desirable aims could be accomplished by measures that are quite within the power of Canada and the jurisdiction of the federal government.

I can almost hear some of you saying: "Doesn't he know that U.S. pilots in the Formosa Straits area are under orders to attack Chinese planes if they interfere with the air-lifting of ammunition to Chiang Kai-shek's troops on the off-shore island and to pursue Communist planes over the Chinese mainland? Doesn't he know that the United Nations Organization rejected India's proposal to put the question of China on the agenda of the General Assembly? Doesn't he know that the Department of Labor at Ottawa fears that during this winter unemployment will be even worse than it was last winter? As for doubling our standard of living, doesn't he know that the economists who advise the federal and provincial governments and the fellows who write in the daily papers about what the economists have to say, are all busy explaining that the present mass unemployment is because we have produced too much of almost everything— especially of the means of production?"

My answer is, yes. I know we are very close to war. Whatever may be the outcome of the present crisis (September 20, 1958) provoked by the Eisenhower administration's determination to maintain military, naval and air bases on Chinese territory, the world will be close to war continuously as long as the U.S. government is permitted to arrogate to itself the authority to threaten with atomic destruction any and every people who attempt to free themselves from enslavement to, or dependence upon, the imperialist powers.

3

I know that rejection of India's resolution by the Steering Committee of the UN demonstrated that the influence of the U.S. government was dominant. But, it illustrated also that its domination is weakening. If you doubt this, consider the following from the special report on the voting by the *New York Times*:

> "*The United States marshalled its voting strength in the Steering Committee today (September 19, 1958) to defeat an Indian move to have the question of Communist Chinese admission to the UN included in the agenda for Assembly debate, but no one could fairly say that it was force of logic that produced the final vote of 12 in favor of the U.S. stand . . .*"

Note well that 12 votes out of 21 was only one more than a bare majority. U.S. dollar domination of the UN is crumbling.

I know that the federal government has been warned that unemployment may be even worse by March, 1959, than it was in March, 1958. I know that in every slump since the war: 1949, 1954 and 1957, the crisis phase of the economic cycle has been worse than it was in the previous slump. I know that this process will continue and get worse unless radical changes are made. But, I know also that we have reached the stage at which radical changes *can* be made. That is the *key* fact.

★   ★   ★

THE need for radical changes in Canada's national policy is admitted now by many who refused to admit it before. For example, the most influential morning newspaper and the most influential evening newspaper in Canada, along with numerous others, are urging the federal government to do some things that were advocated only by the Labor-Progressive Party until a year ago. Recently, a number of representatives of the capitalist class have added their voices to the growing demand for changes in Canada's national policy. Bank presidents, influential industrialists and editors of daily papers, are prominent among the advocates of such changes. Their main immediate emphasis is on the necessity for the

4

government at Ottawa to recognize the tremendous reality of People's China and abandon the silly pretense that Canada can stop, or even obstruct, the Chinese people by refusing to sell them Canadian products that they want to buy.

As Oakley Dalgleish, the editor of the Toronto *Globe and Mail,* said in his speech to the Directors' Luncheon at the Canadian National Exhibition:

"*. . . the present course has done China very little harm and ourselves a great deal of harm. We can't stop China—it may take her a little longer but she will achieve what she wants.*

"*How in the world can a country of 16½ million people, struggling for a place in the world of trade, afford to turn its back on a country of 620 millions who need help, who would accept help and be grateful for it.*"

That statement is an example of the views being presented to boards of trade and chambers of commerce by a growing number of spokesmen for a section of Canadian capital. They don't all emphasize exactly the same opportunities. Some, like A. C. Ashworth and H. R. MacMillan emphasize trade with People's China much as the editor of the *Globe and Mail* does. Others, exemplified by James Muir and Cyrus Eaton, emphasize that our need is for trade with all of the more than 900,000,000 people of the socialist countris. These differences in their approach are not important. What is important is the fact that they are voicing the desires of a growing number of capitalists who want to keep this country under the control of Canadians. Admittedly, they want this for their own selfish reasons. They want to control the very profitable capitalist development of our country and the capitalist exploitation of its people. But, selfish as their capitalist desires may be, their success will strengthen Canada, break down some of the barriers which now divide us from the peoples of the socialist countries. and strengthen the forces for world peace—because it will weaken U.S. dominatioin of our country. Accomplishing that will strengthen the working class.

Attempts are still being made by the apologists for

monopoly-capital to pretend that the potential market for Canadian products in the socialist countries is not very big and does not justify any special effort on Canada's part. Their argument is completely contrary to Canada's interests. Even if the potential of the socialist market were no bigger than its readiness to buy now, it would justify energetic action by Canada to participate in that market to a very much greater extent than at present.

But the argument that the market in the socialist countries is not big and is not likely to grow very much is false; it is directly contrary to well-known facts. For example: it is an established fact that the foreign trade of a country grows with its development of industry. In the light of this fact, consider the following figures of the growth of industry in the socialist countries.

Expansion of industrial production in the first six months of 1958, over the first six months of 1957, was as follows:

People's China, 34%; Korean People's Republic, 34%; Hungarian People's Democratic Republic, 24%; Albanian People's Republic, 19.5%; German Democratic Republic, 11.7% People's Republic of Czechoslovakia, 11%; Polish People's Republic, 10.5%; Soviet Union, 10.7%.

These figures show that the basis of the foreign trade of the socialist countries is growing rapidly. They are going to need more and more machines, more and more specialties, and more and more of the raw materials that they use but do not produce at home. Those Canadian capitalists who are advocating more trade with the socialist countries know what they are talking about.

They Need a New National Policy

ON the surface, it appears that these spokesmen for Canadian capital are simply advocating more foreign trade —with emphasis on the vast new market now developing in China. But, the political essence of their position is that it is a public campaign to arouse the Canadian bourgeoisie.

In general terms and in their proposals for changes in the direction of the policies, which influence the character of Canada's economic development, they are saying: Those of you whose interests are primarily in enterprises owned by Canadians, or which depend upon the development of this country as a distinct economic and political state, must wake up! We must face facts! Look at the opportunities which are inviting us, if we grasp them in time!

Their arguments emphasize the three following main considerations:

- The path to growing overseas markets is open, waiting for us to direct more Canadian trade towards them.

- Expanding trade in overseas markets is essential now if we are to develop heavy industry and finished products manufacturing industries and thereby avoid being reduced to complete dependence on the production of raw materials for the industries of other countries.

- To develop and utilize Canada's enormous resources of industrial raw materials and energy, and to expand our trade, we must avoid world war. Our aim should be peaceful coexistence of states with differing political and economic systems—competition in peace instead of in war.

These three arguments are basic in all the speeches with which representatives of Canadian big business advocate energetic development of trade with the socialist countries. The arguments are logical, they do describe the immediate possibilities to expand Canada's overseas trade; they do describe the path by which the bourgeoisie may yet retain for Canadian capital an effective voice in the real control of Canada as long as capitalism lasts. But, the crux of their position, the hinge on which it turns, is recognition of the necessity to reassert Canada's independence, to discard the policy imposed upon this country under the leadership of Louis St. Laurent. In some of their speeches there peeps out an admission that St. Laurent's policy was contrary to the real interests of Canada and her two peoples, French and English-speaking.

Louis St. Laurent's drive to make our country a producer of raw materials for the U.S., integrated as a dependent satellite in all the aims and policies of U.S. imperialism, was a reactionary attempt to keep Canada out of the mainstream of world democratic progress. St. Laurent did not conceal this fact from the capitalist class. In January, 1947, when he described his reasons for changing the aim upon which Canada's national policy was based, he admitted that his aim was to prepare for a terrible world war "to protect our Christian civilization against the spread of atheistic Communism".

Events proved that St. Laurent was wrong. Disillusionment with the consequences of his policy opened the way for the defeat of his party. John Diefenbaker won the election in June, 1957, by coming before the voters as the man who would put an end to U.S. domination of our country. After winning the election, he continued to pursue the same line introduced by St. Laurent, but in that he is turning away from the very source of his election victories. The Diefenbaker government cannot turn back the clock any more than the government that it defeated could. The growing demands that Canada acts independently of the U.S. are evoked by the needs of Canada, not personal dislike of the U.S. The growth of people's power that Louis St. Laurent feared, has had very much different results from what he anticipated. Instead of being overwhelmed by war, socialism has become the decisive influence in preventing a world war. Canada's need now is to find her place in the new world-wide pattern of peaceful competition.

The most evident reason why Canada needs to grasp the opportunity to seek out a growing role in the changing pattern of world economy is to be seen in the fact that, right now, as this is written, nearly 8% of Canada's workers are unemployed—and this is September, the season of the highest employment. No wonder that the Department of Labor has fear that there may be 1,000,000 workers unemployed by March, 1959.

The crisis phase of the economic cycle which brought this present mass unemployment is markedly different from the minor crises of 1949 and 1954. Then the crisis was limited to North America, today it is spreading all over the capitalist world. Then additional "shots" of inflation produced almost immediate effect in the form of speculative expansion of inventories, expansion of productive capacity, and so on, but this time, inflation has not even maintained the rate of new capital investment, much less brought an increase. Production of the means of production has not yet started to recover.

The policy of so-called "controlled inflation" is becoming bogged down in part of its own consequences; namely, reckless over-expansion of productive capacity in industries producing the means of production. This isn't going to be corrected, not even temporarily, by more inflation; what Canada needs is markets. The capitalists who advocate more energetic action to expand trade with the socialist countries know this. They want to seize the opportunity while it is open to us.

The Age of Great Change

WE are living in an age of great change. Atomic power— and fallout; jet propulsion—and sputniks; the break-up of the old colonial empires—and the changing pattern of world economy and world power: these are expressions of the maturing transformation of both the technical basis and the social forms of civilization.

As this is written (September 20, 1958) it is impossible to forecast in which direction the crisis in the Far East will turn. What is *certain*, is that the Chinese people, sooner or later, will recover control of all their territory. It is impossible that a great nation of 640,000,000 people, recently awakened, developing their country at a speed which has never before been thought possible, and proud of their achievements, will permit continued alienation of their terri-

9

tory and its use for hostile foreign military, naval and air bases.

The incongruity of the U.S. attempt to maintain its grip on Chinese territory makes it hard to believe that the UN General Assembly can sit in full session and permit the U.S. to launch open war. However, if it does, the U.S. defiance of world opinion will evoke such a storm of protest and democratic opposition, including widespread opposition within the United States itself, and boycott of the U.S.A. by numerous peoples, that even the atom-maniacs around President Eisenhower may be forced to halt. Recognition of that, along with the fact that Canada's national interests require trade with People's China, not war, explains why there is arising all across the country a demand that the UN acts to stop U.S. naval and military operations against People's China.

To take the initiative in ending the Far East crisis is part of the golden opportunity that this critical situation offers to Canada. Some influential newspapers drew attention to the significance of this golden opportunity and urged that the Canadian delegation sponsor a proposal to deal with the Far East crisis in the UN. In the House of Commons, Prime Minister Diefenbaker spoke in favor of such action, but then backed away. The Canadian delegation failed to act to end the fighting, on the plea that they had no instructions. This puts our federal government in the camp of those who refuse to act to restore peace in the Far East. This is contrary to the desire of the Canadian people. We know now that war can be prevented. Our national interest requires a policy of *Hands Off People's China!* and energetic action to make that slogan effective.

We must press the federal government now:

—To recognize the People's Government of China and press the expansion of Canadian-Chinese trade.

—Instead of spending $400 million on the development of jet fighter planes which are obsolete before they get into production, the federal government should use the money to finance credits to encourage the export of

*Canada's natural products to China and other countries
of Asia and the socialist world. By this, Canada will "get
in on the ground floor" of the great market which is
going to be the main market of the world within 10
years.*

*—To help prevent world war, and protect the lives
of Canadians and the future of our country, the federal
government should take a public stand now, in favor
of seating China in her rightful place among the other
great states of the world in the United Nations.*

War Is Not Inevitable

THE possibility of preventing war or stopping a war, even
as it is getting started, is one of the big new features
which marks this age of great change. It was illustrated
dramatically when the U.S. government landed marines in
Lebanon and Britain flew troops into Jordan in preparation
for an invasion of Iraq to overthrow its revolutionary government. The world-wide protest, the contradictions of
interest between the imperialist coutries and the strength
of the socialist countries combined to stop the imperialists
in their tracks. Once made aware that, if the U.S.-British
aggression were allowed to continue its consequences would
be atomic war, perhaps on a global scale, and stirred to action
to prevent it, the deep and widespread forces which combined to maintain peace revealed tremendous power.

The U.S. and British troops were stalled. In an
attempt to wriggle out of the dilemma they had created for
themselves the U.S. and British governments united in support of what they called, "the President's Six-Point Plan".
They had it submitted to the UN by President Eisenhower.
That manouevre failed—so completely that they started
arranging another when only three delegates had spoken on
it. Their second scheme was "fronted" by the governments
of Norway, Canada and several other countries. It made
some verbal concessions to the Arab countries, but it failed
also. Both manoeuvres attempted by the U.S. and British
government failed precisely because they sought to avoid

acknowledging the soverign right of the Arab nations each to govern its own country as it sees fit and that the foreign troops should be withdrawn. They were rejected and the resolution introduced by the Arab governments was adopted.

General war in the Middle East was averted at least at that time. Iraq was not invaded, the imperialist troops will be withdrawn. Along with that there was recorded a new and stronger emphasis on the sovereign right of the Arab people to determine their own future and the future of their lands.

That was the third time during the past four years that imperialist instigators of war have been forced to retreat and accept negotiation instead of all-out war as the means by which to deal with disputes. This is a tremendous, and a *historically new,* feature of the conditions of this age.

The first example of this new power was provided when the war in Viet Nam was halted right at the moment when the US. War Department was beginning to take over the direction of the imperialist invasion from the French. The second example was when the British-French-Israeli invasion of Egypt was stopped in 1956; the third was the halting of the U.S.-British plan for the invasion of Iraq in July, 1958.

Each of this triumphs of the people's opposition to war was historic. Combined, they mark a turning point in world development. Many factors combined to make it possible for the forces of peace to stop those who were seeking war, but three factors were outstanding in each. They were:

a) The new tremendous pressure of world opposition to war which confronts the imperialists with mass democratic resistance instead of with easily whipped-up chauvinism.

b) The acute contradictions between the ambitions of aggressive expansionist U.S. imperialism and the older powers that the U.S. is striving to push aside.

c) The historic new state power in the world, the third

of mankind united in the camp of socialism and peace, headed by the mighty Soviet Union. This, the decisive factor in each case, is growing stronger and more potent every day and cannot be separated from the world-wide desire for peace which grows along with it.

This situation illustrates the historic change that has taken place in the relationship of forces in the world. *Objectively* the forces striving to maintain peace have become stronger than those which are seeking to start a war. That is why the decisive events in the world today, the main direction of developments, strengthen the possibility that world war will be prevented.

This doesn't mean that there is no longer any danger of world war. The fact is that, for the time being, it makes those who favor war more reckless than ever — for example, the manner in which John Foster Dulles commited the U.S. to fight if necessary to prevent People's China from occupying islands that are within less than three miles of the mainland coast — closer than Prince Edward Island is to any other part of Canada or Vancouver Island is to Vancouver. That is why Mao Tse-tung and Nikita Khrushchev pointed out in their joint statement on this matter:

"The aggressive circles of the western powers are to this day refusing to take any real measures to safeguard peace and, on the contrary, are insensately aggravating international tension, are placing mankind on the brink of military catastrophes."

The Path to Disaster

NATIONAL policies geared to preparations for war are, in effect, shortsighted attempts to deny the realities of this age of change.

For example, consider the special meeting of the federal cabinet on Sunday, September 20.

According to press reports one of the questions before the members of the government at that meeting was: What to do about the Arrow? The Arrow is the experimental prototype of a jet-propelled fighter plane developed by

Avro corporation for the RCAF. Is is reported in the press that $400 million have been spent on the development of this prototype. In the process the A. V. Roe Company has become one of the richest corporations in Canada. If the plane is not put into large-scale production to be used by the RCAF, that $400 million will have been wasted (like so many other hundreds of millions that have been spent on preparation for war). But, to put the plane into large-scale production will entail expeditures totalling more than $2,000 million — for a plane which will be obsolete before enough have been built to equip one squadron.

This is an example of the manner in which $1800 million a year, nearly half of all the revenues of the federal government, have been spent through the past 10 years. It is a waste of all the surplus produced by the Canadian workers and farmers. To make it appear that this senseless waste created prosperity the government has resorted to inflation so that our money buys less every year than it would pay for the year before. Indeed, this insane, suicidal armament binge without heavier taxation of profits, can be maintained only by inflation. The result for the people is illustrated by the fact that today it requires two dollars to buy what one dollar would buy even during the war, in spite of the fact that then there was a drastic scarcity of almost everything, while today the warehouses are choked with unsold products.

Inflation has been a constant feature of the insane policy of gearing the economy of Canada to the suicidal aims of U.S. imperialism.

The Diefenbaker government, through Bank of Canada operations, has speeded up the rate of inflation substantially during this year, especially since the federal election. During the first six months of this year the volume of government securities held by the chartered banks was increased by more than $600 million, or 24 percent. The total money supply, in the form of currency and bank money, was increased by 3 percent within three months of the federal election. The value of every life insurance policy has been cut, the purchasing power of pensions, savings deposits, family allowances and all fixed incomes, have been reduced. All this because of the government's subordination of Canada's national interests to preparing for world war.

The demoralizing effect of inflation can be seen in the rapid growth of speculation and economic parasitism. On every stock exchange speculators are gambling on continued decline in the value of Canada's money, a continued increase in the cost of living, and increasing skepticism about the stability of the financial system.

During the recent increase in the speed of inflation in Canada and the U.S., there appeared on the stock markets a phenomenon which previously had been considered to belong only to the capitalist countries of Europe (and to China under Chiang Kai-shek). Market prices of shares in corporations rose, in the face of declining production, sales, and profits, in what some economists describe as a "stampede from the dollar". A prominent U.S. financier said recently, "... *few people any longer believe that our currency can ever be worth more in terms of buying power and most likely it will ultimately be worth considerably less.*" (Toronto Daily Star, August 25, 1958.)

What Should We Do?

A number of people tend to agree that enormous expenditures on armaments to the accompaniment of infation is suicidal and should be stopped, — and then to ask: "But, do you want economic crisis and unemployment? How else can the government provide jobs?"

The answer is that armaments and inflation have not prevented economic crisis and mass unemployment; they've made them worse. As for the second part of the question, consider how much more employment would have been created and how much more real, lasting benefit would have been secured if, instead of spending $400 million developing a jet fighter plane which was obsolete before it got into production, the government had established credits for the export of Canada's natural products to China; or if this money had been invested as the federal government's share in financing the development of the enormous power resources of the Columbia River. Abundant and cheap hydro electrical energy in the midst of the wealth of industrial raw materials would bring scores of industries to the interior of British Columbia within a few years.

The Columbia River watershed and the tremendous possibilities that await its development is but an example of scores of great undertakings that should be carried out in Canada. Development of the hydro-electrical power potential of the Grand Falls on the Hamilton River in Quebec; building the Chignecto Canal; reforestation of the eastern slopes of the Rockies with the necessary works to conserve and utilize the headwaters of the great rivers which rise there; the building of petro-chemical industries to utlize the unmeasured resources of oil and natural gas and coal of western Canada, are a few other examples. Such long-term development works will provide the market for an expanded steel and machine-building industry, and for the raw materials that we cannot export; employment for engineers and technicians, as well as for tens of thousands of mechanics and laborers. Only by such large-scale development can Canada's economy, cities, educational opportunities, and living standards, rise in an all-sided way.

What will we do with the enormously increased production? We shall need it for export. Doubling our living standard will involve doubling our foreign trade.

We can double our living standards, reduce the working week to 32 hours per week, provide opportunities for every talented youngster to receive higher education to the full extent that he or she pursues it, and for elderly people to retire with adequate pensions while they are still young enough to enjoy the fruitful creative use of leisure. All these possibilities invite us. To make them into reality requires that we withdraw from the suicidal effort of U.S. imperialism to turn the clock back; that we adopt instead a national policy based on the perspective of long-term peaceful coexistence of states with differing political and economic systems.

Life or death for perhaps millions of us who live here depends upon this issue. The manner and direction of U.S. policy and even more so, of U.S. war preparations, even those on Canadian territory, show that a world war would include war of nuclear missiles and attempts at airborne attack and counter-attack across the Arctic.

With the new means of horrible mass slaughter and destruction, widespread devastation which would render big areas uninhabitable for a century and contaminate the atmosphere permanently, Canada and her people would be the very first victims of any such war.

One of the lessons to be learned from U.S. behavior until now is that it would almost certainly mean the end of all hopes of regaining our national independence.

In striking contrast to that prospect of physical and national destruction, peaceful coexistence with the socialist states offers Canada bright prospects for trade and continued economic expansion in peace. Development of relations of peaceful coexistence will enable Canada again to export her products to the countries which are in the sterling area as well as to the socialist countries. It will enable Canada to take advantage of her closeness to Asia across the Pacific. Canadian industry will have full opportunity to participate in the coming imminent era of the industrialization of Asia. Every consideration of national interests urges Canadians to strive for peaceful coexistence, to decide the contest between the socialist and capitalist systems of society by peaceful coexistence, not by war.

In addition to the fact that it is our sole alternative to physical and national destruction, peaceful coexistence of states with differing political and economic systems is the path along which the Canadian people will achieve continued progress and a better life.

Capitalist Parties Won't Do It!

CANADA'S national independence has been wantonly sacrificed during the past 10 years. The U.S.A. has been allowed, nay, helped to gain control of our country by occupying U.S. armed forces. To continue along this path would mean to abandon entirely the dream of developing our country as an independent, industrially developed, state.

The national policy by which we can develop our country for the benefit of her people, in peace, is the policy of national independence—the policy of active economic, cultural, and political intercourse with every country with which such intercourse is mutually desired and advantageous. To develop such a policy requires, at the very least, recognition of the fact that the best interests of Canada require that the central contradiction of this epoch, the contradiction between the socialist world system and the imperialist world system, be solved in peaceful competition—not by war. Canada's independence must be reasserted by us taking an honorable place in the new pattern of world trade and world political relationships.

This is a challenge to the labor movement as well as an opportunity, because our national independence will be regained only when, and to the extent that, Labor steps forward in Canadian political life as an independent political force, demanding an end to U.S. domination of our country.

Truly Canadian policies will be introduced only as a result of the pressure of the working class and its democratic allies. Neither the Liberal party nor the Progressive-Conservative party will do it—particularly as long as they are allowed to continue to exercise unchallenged monopoly of the House of Commons and the government of Canada. It must be admitted also that the CCF until now has supported their policies.

The inability of either of the two old parties of Canadian capitalism to reassert the national independence of our two peoples, is illustrated by their irresponsible betrayal of our independence since the second world war.

Louis St. Laurent sacrificed Canada's independence for integration in the war plan of U.S. imperialism without ever telling the people that he was doing it. Lester Pearson, who was the main personal instrument by which St. Laurent operated his subordination of Canada to the U.S.A., put forward proposals in his federal election campaign in March, 1958, which were in effect a repudiation of Louis St. Laurent's policy. During the session of the House of Commons which followed the election, Lester Pearson repeated those proposals. But, he did not once consider it necessary to acknowledge that they were different in their essential content than were the policies of the government of which he was previously a member. The general attitude is that: "Then I was a member of the government; now I am in opposition."

John Diefenbaker illustrates the same type of political thinking—moving in the other direction; namely, from opposition into governmental office. In the federal general election campaign of June, 1957, he found wide circles of people openly resentful of the effects of U.S. domination of Canada and demanding new national policies. Discarding the elaborate Tory platform that had been adopted by the convention which elected him leader of the party John Diefenbaker listened to the people and gave voice to some of their desires. As a result of that, he appeared to the voters as the man who would put an end to the "tight money" policy introduced by the Liberals, stop the sell-out to the U.S., re-establish a reasonable balance between overseas markets and the U.S. in Canada's foreign trade, revive the development of secondary industries in Canada and reassert Canada's sovereignty over her armed forces and her territory. Hundreds of thousands of the voters who helped to elect Diefenbaker candidates did so entirely on the basis of one or more of these expectations.

What has Prime Minister Diefenbaker done? He has continued to condemn the Liberals, but in the main he continues to pursue the policies for which he condemns them. Instead of reducing interest rates, his government has increased the interest rate on more than a third of the whole of Canada's national debt, from 3% to 4½%. He has adopted inflation as a long-term policy; he has given rich capitalist interests a 50% increase in their claims against the taxpayers.

He promised to divert 15% of Canada's foreign trade away from the U.S.A. to British Commonwealth markets, but in the Commonwealth trade conference, which is in progress in Montreal as this is being written, the Canadian delegation has represented the interests of the U.S. dollar bloc, pretending that recovery of trade is waiting for Britain to guarantee the pound freely convertible into dollars. To have implemented the prime minister's promise would have meant that Canada would undertake to defy the U.S. and accept payment for exports in sterling.

Prime Minister Diefenbaker promised to make companies incorporated in Canada responsible solely to Canadian law. When President Eisenhower addressed a joint session of the House of Commons and the Senate in Ottawa, he dealt with that proposal and rejected it. His categoric refusal was off-hand, almost disdainful. The *Financial Post* described it as a dose of "shock treatment." But Mr. Diefenbaker accepted it obediently, exactly as the Liberals have done so many times before him.

As for restoring Canada's sovereignty, one of the first acts of the Diefenbaker government was to barter away Canada's command of the RCAF to the U.S. commander of the North American Air Command. On Wednesday, August 13, Mr. Alvin Hamilton, Minister of Northern Affairs, admitted that even he, the "Minister of the Crown," cannot visit the vast territories for which he is supposed to be responsible without first getting permission from the U.S.A. The minister admitted ruefully that on one occasion it took so long to secure permission for an employee to go to the north country in connection with the work of his department that the man left his job before permission was secured.

In the sphere of foreign policy, John Diefenbaker declared that Canada would pursue a clearly defined Canadian foreign policy.

What has he done? In the Middle East, for example? First, the prime minister assured President Eisenhower that the U.S. would have Canada's support in its invasion of the Middle East. Then, he said in the House of Commons, "I trust that a prompt and positive reply will be forthcoming to Premier Khrushchev's proposal. There should be a summit meeting as soon as possible." The next day, when Macmillan and Eisenhower put forward their trick proposal for the Middle East crisis to be dealt with in the UN Security Council, Prime Minister Diefenbaker switched again and supported that.

Referring to the crisis provoked by the U.S. 7th Fleet in the Formosa straits the prime minister told the members of the House of Commons on September 6, "I think the world wants to be assured that nothing will be left undone to prevent any action that might result in the world sliding into disastrous consequences. . . . As far as Canada is concerned, I think Canadians as a whole would expect that their representatives will not fail at this time to explore every avenue for the settlement of the grave situation which today prevails, and it is in that spirit that I suggest the UN might have an opportunity and an appointment with responsibility in this direction." (House of Commons Debates, September 6, 1958, p. 4703.)

If the assurance implicit in those words had been made good Canada would have been a co-sponsor with India of the proposal to place the question before the UN General Assembly. But the Canadian delegation pleaded that it "had no instructions." Harold Greer, the experienced correspondent of the *Toronto Daily Star* at the UN, explained it differently. He wrote that the directives received from Ottawa by the delegation "appear to run counter to Prime Minister

Diefenbaker's belief that the Formosa crisis should be referred to the UN General Assembly."

That sort of on again, off again, somersaulting is becoming characteristic of Prime Minister Diefenbaker.

All the way along he has exposed the Liberals and condemned them—and then he has continued, with minor variations, to do what he had condemned the Liberals for doing.

But the inconsistencies, the difference between words and deeds, the political gyrations, are not the result of personal peculiarities of Prime Minister Diefenbaker. The problem confronting Canadian democracy does not flow out of differences between Tory and Liberal prime ministers—in fact, as shown above, there is no really basic difference between them. Like his dramatic success in two federal elections, Prime Minister Diefenbaker's political inconsistencies mirror the deepening contradictions within the capitalist class. Contradictory attitudes to U.S. domination, speculations on what the United States might do, half-hearted attempts to develop Canadian policies—an acute and increasingly evident contradiction between their greed for the "killings" that may be made immediately in the sell-out of Canada to the U.S.A. and their desire to maintain for themselves an influential voice in the capitalist monopoly control of Canada: this contradiction is both the characteristic and the dilemma of Canadian capitalists as a class.

Our country needs a radical change in its national policies. Many Canadian recognize this; some of them are working consistently to bring it about. Among them are some representatives of the capitalist class. To some extent, John Diefenbaker's overwhelming victory in the federal general election also was a result of this recognition. But the change made by the elections was only from the smugly complacent conservatism of the Liberal capitalist lawyer, Louis St. Laurent, to the Tory capitalist lawyer, John Diefenbaker.

The political parties of monopoly-capital will not stop U.S. domination of Canada.

Canadian monopoly-capital is linked by innumerable interlocking interests and directorates with U.S. monopolies in Canada and in the U.S.A. The operations of Canadian monopolies are integral with the struggle to maintain monopoly-capitalism against the turbulent historical tide of democratic change which characterizes this new epoch.

Political action to stop the U.S. domination of Canada is action against the imperialist drive for war; it is action in the direction of taking Canada out of the war camp.

The most that the people of Canada can count upon is that the capitalist class will divide on the issue of national independence versus U.S. domination. The number of capitalists who will support the struggle for policies of Canadian independence, and their political weight, will be determined by the strength of the overall support for the demand. In the main, members of the capitalist class are more anxious to increase their profits than to be right.

Labor's Opportunity

TO stop U.S. domination of our country and to bring about the sort of policies that are needed now in domestic affairs requires the bringing together of a political force which is not hamstrung by ties with U.S. imperialism, as both the Liberal and Tory parties are. It must represent the interests of the masses of the people and be able to unite them at the polls.

The core of such a political force must be the more advanced, politically active members of the working class, but the movement as a whole will not necessarily be committed to the abolition of capitalism. A broad People's Democratic Political Movement, today, will be a reform movement, proposing far-reaching changes, but not a fundamental transformation of society. That is, as yet, the nature of political thinking in the labor movement, and among wide circles of forward-looking Canadians. In this sense it can be said that, in the problems that it is bringing forward in domestic policy as well as in foreign relations, Canada's Opportunity is Labor's Opportunity.

Now is the time for the trade unions to step forward as the organized basis of a great People's Political Movement.

The conditions demand such a movement. The terms of the resolution on Political Action, adopted by the Canadian Labor Congress at its Winnipeg Convention, describe, exactly, such a movement as suits the conditions of today.

The resolution adopted by the Winnipeg convention of the Canadian Labor Congress sets before the labor movement the task of bringing together in united parliamentary action, *"an effective alternative political force based on the needs of workers, farmers and similar groups . . . interested in basic social reforms and reconstruction through our parliamentary system of governments."*

The above is definite enough to specify the interests to be served, and at the same time it is broad enough to embrace all progressive forces, including the Labor-Progressive Party.

Contrary to the assertions of some spokesmen of the CCF, some of whom are officers of the CLC, the carefully drafted resolution adopted by the Winnipeg convention did not exclude Communists from the projected new movement, either as individuals or as a party, because it states specifically that the forms of organization developed should provide *"for the broadest possible participation of all individuals and groups."*

The Labor-Progressive Party solidarized itself with that sentiment in its public statement greeting the Winnipeg resolution. The LPP said:

> *"Canadian Communists have advocated exactly such a concept continuously since the day that we founded the Workers' Party of Canada in the Labor Temple on Church Street, Toronto, in 1922. It was the central proposal that the LPP placed before the electorate in the recent federal general election. It is right at the centre of the LPP proposal, in our national program, for the development of independent working class political action and labor-farmer unity. The outcome of the federal general election shows clearly that such action, now envisaged by the CLC, is an urgent necessity for all*

24

workers, farmers, and forward-looking professional people."

While emphasizing, without any equivocation, its agreement with, and support for, the aim proclaimed in the resolution adopted by the Canadian Labor Congress convention the LPP has found it necessary to draw attention to the fact that many of the public statements of the national leaders of the CCF are in direct contradiction to the terms of the resolution.

They Misrepresent the Winnipeg Convention

THE main political line of the official propaganda of the national officers of the CCF is to the effect that the executive officers of the Canadian Labor Congress are planning to continue the mistaken and unsuccessful policy of the old Canadian Congress of Labor of tieing the trade union movement financially for political action to the CCF. Some of the national leaders of the CCF say this plainly; it was boasted about in the CCF national convention.

This is directly contrary to the text and the spirit of the CLC resolution. The Winnipeg convention adopted an imaginative proposal, projecting a united effort which corresponds with the political state of mind of the labor movement as a whole and broad circles of democratic farmers, cooperators, and other middle class people. Their general political state of mind is characterized by unity in their desire for reforms. They want meansures to raise living standards, strengthen the trade union movement, broaden opportunities, provide social security for all and to maintain peace, but they are not agreed that any one of the existing political parties is the sole instrument by which it is to be accomplished, or should be given control of the political movement which will accomplish them. The broad People's Political Movement envisaged in the resolution adopted by the Winnipeg convention provides exactly the means by which reform-minded people with different organizational affiliations can cooperate in elections to achieve unity at the polls.

25

The right-wing leaders of the CCF and a number of CCF'ers in strategic trade union positions are misrepresenting that proposal by referring to it as though it had been an unprincipled trick resolution to screen the shackling of the trade unions politically to the CCF. For example, they are declaring in British Columbia that the purpose of the Winnipeg resolution was to elect a CCF government in that province. In the first political action conference convened at the call of the B.C. Federation of Labor the delegates were informed by a trade union official who is also a prominent CCF'er that the conference was not called to discuss the resolution adopted at the Winnipeg convention of the Canadian Labor Congress. "We are not here to discuss setting up a united front, we are here to . . .elect a CCF government in B.C."

No official spokesman of the Canadian Labor Congress has verified these CCF statements. Claude Jodoin, President of the Canadian Labor Congress, addressed the National Convention of the CCF and he did not indicate that he agreed that the words of the resolution adopted by the CLC convention in Winnipeg were, in fact, only a screen for the shackling of the Canadian Labor Congress to the CCF. But it is significant that he did not specifically dissociate himself from that CCF claim, although it had been made repeatedly in the CCF convention.

Fight for the Winnipeg Resolution

THE Labor-Progressive Party has no narrow partisan interest in pointing out that the labor movement as a whole can only lose by such ambiguity. The trade union movement cannot unite its own ranks to win elections, either provincially or federally, if it demands that its members vote only for the candidates selected by the CCF. The members of the unions in each constituency must be given a share in choosing candidates—as well as in financing their campaign.

The majority of the political active workers of the trade union movement want that. A large number of rank and file members of the CCF want that, recognizing that it is the one means by which a Labor-Farmer majority can be elected federally and in most of the provinces. Tens of thousands of farmers will support this proposal. The need is for all of us who support this idea to fight to make it a reality.

The LPP approaches the possibility of organizing a democratic people's political movement exactly in accord with the text of the resolution adopted by the Winnipeg convention of the Canadian Labor Congress—and in the spirit in which the delegates there voted for it.

The resolution quite distinctly calls for the bringing together in united political action of trade unions, farm organizations, cooperatives and democratic parties and individuals who support the program of the movement and desire to join forces to give it effect. The resolution specifically subordinates the question of structure to the necessity of bringing together all the organizations and individuals willing to act. The LPP will help to accomplish that—at all levels of electoral action. It will fight to be a part of the new people's political movement right from the beginning. LPP members will initiate discussions in their local unions, in political action committees, preliminary conferences such as the conferences being organized by provincial Federations of Labor and will insist upon participation by the LPP in making the actual arrangements for unity at the polls.

Workers who have not voted for the CCF until now will not be tricked into voting CCF by double-talk. Aside from that, history has shown already that conditions in our country require a Canadian organizational approach to the problem.

As Canadian Communists pointed out when we were building the Canadian Labor Party years ago (the Canadian Labor Party was destroyed in 1927 when the Executive Council of the AFL ordered its affiliated locals and central councils in Canada to withdraw from the Canadian Labor Party or face expulsion from the AFL) Canadian conditions require that a democratic people's political movement shall provide a type of organization within which forward-looking political activists can cooperate for the achievement of immediate political objectives by affiliation of their local unions, cooperatives or political parties and participation by all affiliated bodies in the selection of candidates, etc. (*Steps to Power,* 1925.) That cannot be achieved if the idea of independent labor political action is narrowed down to support of CCF candidates.

The CCF surrendered its claim (or pretense) to be a party fighting for a socialist Canada when it supplanted the Regina Manifesto by its "Winnipeg Declaration." The CCF supported St. Laurent in integrating Canada in the war drive of U.S. imperialism, in committing Canada to NATO, and in cutting Canada off from a big part of her overseas markets by pointing the U.S. dollar bloc. The CCF's record of opportunist association with the very policies that now must be discarded and reversed, is itself a conclusive reason why the people's poliitcal movement proposed by the Winnipeg convention of the Canadian Labor Congress must, genuinely, be new and broader than the CCF. It must unite for political action all the progressive forces in Canada.

Canada's Party of Socialism

THE Labor-Progressive Party is the party of the struggle for socialism. This struggle includes the development of united independent working class political action. To help develop united action we will cooperate in every way to organize electoral action on the lines described by the resolution on Political Action adopted by the Winnipeg convention. The LPP will support electoral agreements, electoral alliances and more permanent forms of election unity. The only condition that the LPP attaches to its support is that the action be directed to the development of an all-inclusive electoral alternative to the Liberal and Conservative parties, as called for in the Winnipeg resolution of the CLC. Subject to that condition, members of the LPP will do everything in their power to develop consistent fraternal electoral cooperation with supporters of the CCF—and with all forward-looking people.

Members of the LPP will advocate all-inclusive conferences of trade unions and other organizations which accept the legislative program of the Canadian Labor Congress. In such conferences, members of the LPP will urge their fellow delegates to stay by the spirit of the Winnipeg convention and the letter of its resolution. Our aim is to work with all progressive forces in developing systematic discussion of that resolution and going forward in united action to give organizational form to the grand democratic idea that it describes.

★   ★   ★

WE ARE living in a new epoch of sweeping political and economic change. It is the epoch of the world-wide transition to socialism. National liberation struggles are making an end of the empires, the imperialist system is in a profound crisis, the idea of socialism has seized the imagination of the majority of mankind. In this crisis, Canada has a golden opportunity—to help prevent a world war, to expand her industries and her trade and to enrich the lives of all her people.

The majority of Canadians want peace and trade and democratic progress, but to achieve it Canada needs the development of a united People's Political Movement, rallied around the organized labor movement, united in independent labor political action. The building of such a movement is an indispensable part of the historic advance of the working people: to political action independent of the capitalist class, against the stranglehold of the monopolies and their senior partner, U.S. imperialism, to national independence and the flowering of Canadian development—in peace.

It is by such political action that the working class of the two peoples of our country, French and English-speaking, will win their way to the leadership of their nations.

DATE DUE / DATE DE RETOUR

Subscribe to These
Marxist Journals

WORLD MARXIST REVIEW

Published each month. A political journal of the world's Communist parties.

SUBSCRIPTION RATES: $3.50 YEARLY.

FILL OUT FORM:
PROGRESS BOOKS
924 King St. W., Toronto, Ont.

I wish to subscribe to World Marxist Review. I enclose $3.50 for a year's subscription.

Name ....

Address ....

MARXIST REVIEW

Monthly political journal of
Labor-Progressive Party.

SUBSCRIPTION — 8 issues (each 2 months) for $2.00;
6 issues $1.50.

MARXIST REVIEW
24 Cecil St., Toronto, Ont.

I wish to subscribe to Marxist Review, I enclose $ ....

Name ....

Address ....

9 781015 241879